Sports Illustrated
FOOTBALL: DEFENSE

The Sports Illustrated Library

BOOKS ON TEAM SPORTS

Baseball   Football: Defense   Ice Hockey
Basketball   Football: Offense   Volleyball
Curling

BOOKS ON INDIVIDUAL SPORTS

Badminton   Horseback Riding   Tennis
Fly Fishing   Skiing   Track and Field: Running Events
Golf   Squash   Wrestling

BOOKS ON WATER SPORTS

Junior Sailing   Swimming and Diving
Powerboating   Small Boat Sailing
Skin Diving and Snorkeling

SPECIAL BOOKS

Dog Training   Safe Driving

Sports Illustrated
FOOTBALL:
DEFENSE

BY BUD WILKINSON

**Illustrations
by Robert Handville**

J. B. LIPPINCOTT COMPANY
Philadelphia and New York

U.S. Library of Congress Cataloging in Publication Data

Wilkinson, Charles Burnham.
    Sports illustrated football: defense.

    (The Sports illustrated library)
    1. Football-Defense.   I. Sports illustrated
(Chicago)   II. Title.
GV951.1.W54 1973   796.33'22   73–9617
ISBN–0–397–00833–3
ISBN–0–397–00993–3 (pbk.)

Cover photograph: Al Freni.

Photograph on page 8: Al Freni.

Photographs on pages 38, 44 and 54: Vernon J. Biever.

Contents

Sports Illustrated
FOOTBALL: DEFENSE

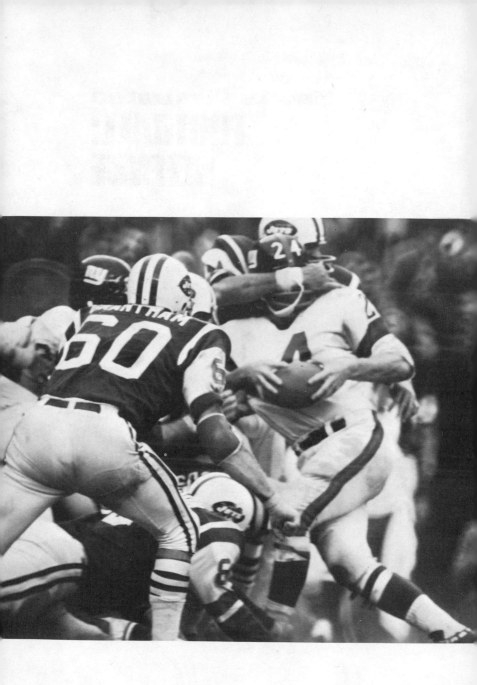

Introduction

ON MANY AN AUTUMN Saturday, in places like Norman and Tuscaloosa, Columbus and Ann Arbor, the chant echoes through a packed football stadium: "Dee-fense! Dee-fense!" And on Sundays, too, among the professionals from Yankee Stadium to Wrigley Field to the Los Angeles Coliseum, the cry is the same. The fans have finally caught onto something. They have grasped one of the essentials—perhaps *the* essential—of the game. Defense is what really wins it.

A perfect defense means that the other team doesn't score, and nobody ever lost a football game when the other team had a zero on the scoreboard.

While the defense is at last beginning to come into its own, winning long-deserved recognition from fans and sportswriters alike, it is still true, and perhaps always will be, that the offensive stars—the quarterbacks, the breakaway runners and the speedy pass-catching ends—receive the greater attention and acclaim. Perhaps there is something deep-rooted in the psychology of it that grants more recognition to the player who scores points than to the player who prevents the scoring of points. To some, there will always seem a bit of negativism attached to the defense, but the knowledgeable football man will never accept that argument. He fully appreciates that it requires a great deal of skill and creativity to stop the other side from scoring touchdowns.

From a tactical and strategic standpoint, football can be divided into three phases: (1) the offense, (2) the defense and (3) the kicking game. One way of reemphasizing the importance of the defense is to consider the two ways a team gets possession of the ball: (1) by stopping the opponents and forcing them to surrender the ball after four downs, or (2) by receiving a kickoff after the opponents have scored. It is self-evident that any team that leads the league in number of kickoff returns is not going to have a winning record.

Each of the three phases of football requires outstanding athletic ability, but most coaches agree that playing effective defense takes far more physical ability than any other phase. Primarily, this is because playing defense calls for an immediate response to an unknown situation. Offense is, by contrast, a relatively static situation in which players execute precisely defined assignments.

On defense, all players are confronted with the following problems on every play:

(1) *Where to line up*. Since different offensive formations have different areas of strength, defensive men are not sure about the position they must take until the offensive team has taken its own position. Therefore, the defense must adjust its alignment to meet the strength of the offensive formation.

(2) *The defense is handicapped at the START of each play*. The offensive team knows *when* the ball will be snapped, and by proper execution of the starting count, it can beat the defensive team to the punch at the

start of each play. Thus, when the play begins, the defensive team is momentarily behind.

(3) *Offensive plays are designed to mislead the defense.* All of the maneuvers and fakes of the offensive team are executed to fool the defense regarding the real point of attack. If a defensive player is drawn out of position, even for a split second, the offense has gained another great advantage.

To summarize: the defensive player does not know *where* he will line up. He will be slightly *behind* at the start of every play. And after surrendering these two advantages, he must *ignore the fakes of the offense*, move to the ball and stop the play for no gain. All this requires tremendous athletic ability.

By way of contrast, the offensive player knows before the play begins:

(1) Exactly *where* he will line up.

(2) Exactly *when* the ball will be snapped.

(3) Precisely *what* his assignment will be on the play.

Thus, the offensive situation is totally static. It requires little in the way of reaction. Given average ability, a boy can be taught through proper practice and repetitive drills to become an effective offensive player. Because of the difficult physical and mental reactions that are necessary to play defense, however, it is impossible for a boy who does not possess outstanding ability to become an effective defensive player.

This raises interesting coaching problems. How do you place your players in position? Who will be your offensive linemen, defensive linemen, linebackers, offensive backs, wide receivers, etc.? The judgment involved in these decisions is most difficult for the coach. Because of the glamour of offense, the natural coaching reaction is to place the best athletes on the offensive unit and then piece together the defensive unit from the talent that remains.

However, assuming defense is the most important phase of the game, and that it requires superior ability, then the best athletes should be assigned to the defensive unit. The offensive team will consequently be manned by the most effective athletes remaining after the defensive team has been set. (Offensive quarterback may be the exception.)

In assigning squad members to various positions, physical factors are paramount. The question arises whether speed and quickness are more important than size and weight, or vice versa. Generally, it is more important on defense to have speed and quickness than size and weight. Defensive players must hit, react and then use their speed to move to the ball. Football is primarily a game of reaction and speed of foot, and defensive players who lack quickness and speed surrender the basic ingredient of successful defensive play. It is obvious, however, that if the speed-quickness factor is equal, the bigger and heavier men will play better than smaller men.

The mental attitude of defensive players is also vitally important. They must be highly aggressive—physical fighters. One of the axioms of football is that on each play "you either hit or get hit." The players who "get hit'" are the ones who lose. Since the defensive team is behind at the start of the play because of the offense's knowledge of the starting count, it must be aggressive enough to hit, fight and overcome this disadvantage with its willpower, determination and physical skills. The defense must be prepared to "outhit" its opponents if it expects to stop them.

What follows is a basic text designed to explain the mechanics and theory of defensive football to young players, coaches at the cub-football or junior-high level and those fans who desire a more complete understanding of the game.

1

Components
of the
Defensive Team

THERE ARE MANY different defensive patterns or alignments. However, every team defensive alignment is made up of the same basic components. These are:

(1) Down or interior linemen.
(2) Defensive ends.
(3) Linebackers.
(4) Secondary men.

In some situations, the defensive pattern being used requires a single player to execute the fundamentals of two of the above positions.

Interior or down linemen take their position within a yard of the line of scrimmage from offensive tackle to offensive tackle. The term "down" derives from the fact that they have one or both hands on the ground as they take their stance.

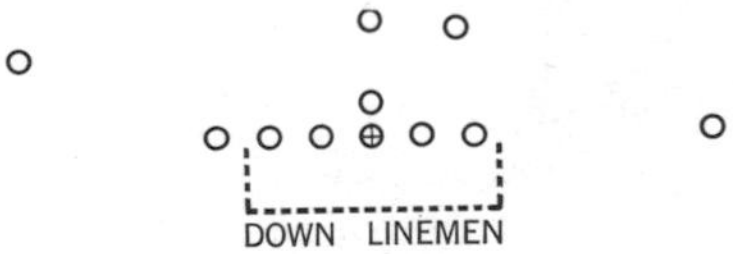

DOWN LINEMEN

Diagram 1

Defensive ends take their position within 1 yard of the line of scrimmage head up with, on the outside shoulder of or just outside the offensive tackle or end.

DEFENSIVE ENDS
Diagram 2

Linebackers take their position 1½ yards to 3½ yards behind the line of scrimmage, head up with the offensive tight ends or inside of them.

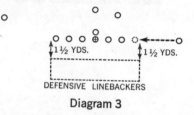

DEFENSIVE LINEBACKERS

Diagram 3

The rules prohibit the interior offensive linemen from moving further than 1 yard downfield on pass plays. By lining up at least 1½ yards behind the line of scrimmage and watching (or "keying" on) the linemen, the backers get a quick indication of whether the play is a pass or a run, since the offensive linemen cannot cross the line to block them on pass plays.

Secondary men take their position 2 to 8 yards behind the line of scrimmage when they are playing against a wide receiver, and from 6 to 12 yards behind the line when they are deployed to defend against the inside strength of an offensive formation.

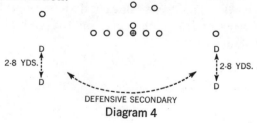

DEFENSIVE SECONDARY
Diagram 4

2

Basic Fundamentals of Defensive Football

DEFENSIVE MEN in close proximity to offensive players (interior linemen or defensive ends) must charge, hit their opponent with enough force to neutralize his charge, control the opponent to avoid being blocked, locate the ball and then move to it. To do all these things in a few seconds takes great athletic ability, and to do them consistently throughout a game takes the skills of a Mike Reid, a Claude Humphrey or a Mean Joe Greene.

DEFENSIVE KEYS

Men who take their position further than 1½ yards from any offensive player (linebackers and secondary men) must "read" or "key" as the ball is snapped. These terms mean watching one or two offensive players whose movement at the start of the play usually indicates the type of play to be run.

15

Since the rules prevent the offensive tackles, guards or center from being more than a yard across the line of scrimmage on forward pass plays, the moment an ineligible receiver moves further than a yard downfield, the defense can safely assume that the play is a run and close to stop the ball carrier.

By watching the offensive linemen and reading the following keys, linebackers and secondary men can learn the type and/or direction of the play:

(1) Offensive linemen downfield means the play is a run.

(2) Offensive linemen pulling out either to the left or right indicates that the play is going in that direction. (Occasionally the linemen may pull in the wrong direction to mislead the defense.)

(3) Offensive linemen drop-stepping back to execute a pass-protection block indicates that the play will be a pass. (On occasion, they will use this movement when the play is a draw play or a screen pass.)

Diagram 5

Illus. 1. Linebacker ready to key Number 75.

A. Offensive lineman charges across line of scrimmage. Play is a run. Linebacker penetrates.

B. Lineman pulls to the left. Linebacker moves to the left.

C. Lineman pulls to the right. Linebacker moves to the right.

D. Lineman drop-steps to make a pass-protection block. Linebacker drops to his zone.

It is vitally important that men who are keying do not become overanxious and move too quickly in the wrong direction. A step in the wrong direction requires another step to put the player back in his original position. Thus, two steps have been wasted, which will delay the defensive player's ability to get to the ball. And since football is a game of inches and split seconds, this can sometimes mean the difference between victory and defeat.

Diagram 6A   Diagram 6B

To avoid moving in the wrong direction, linebackers and secondary men should take a short drop step with either foot while they read the movement of the offensive linemen. By doing this, they will hold their position until they are sure of the type of play being run, instead of advancing the wrong way.

BLOCK PROTECTION

The most important fundamental for all defensive players is "block protection." To move to the ball, defensive players must keep their legs free. If an offensive man is successful in getting to the defender's legs or body, he can effectively block the defender and prevent his further movement in the direction of the ball.

Proper block protection requires that, immediately before contact with an offensive blocker, the defensive player have his feet spread about the width of his shoulders, his knees bent and his hands and arms dangling down to protect his knees, thighs and waist. (See Illustration

18

2.) From this position, the defender can deliver a blow with his hands, arms and shoulders to knock the offensive player away from his legs and body and thereby maintain freedom of movement.

Illus. 2. Block protection hitting position.

Improper block protection results from the defensive player *not* bending his knees enough to lower his center of gravity and enable him to deliver an up-and-out blow. His hands and arms are now so high that the blocker can get under the block protection to the defender's legs and body to make an effective block. (See Illustration 3.) Another block-protection error is to have the feet

Illus. 3. Defensive player is too high and blocker gets to his body.

too close together. This eliminates the balance and body control needed to fight the opponent and again raises the defender's center of gravity. (See Illustration 4.)

Illus. 4. Defensive player's feet are too close together.

PROPER ANGLE OF PURSUIT

After diagnosing the play and locating the ball, all defensive players must move to the ball on the "proper angle of pursuit." The correct angle is the course the defender must take to meet the ball carrier at the earliest possible moment.

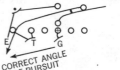

Diagram 7

The relative speeds of the two men is the controlling factor. The faster the ball carrier, the further downfield the defensive lineman or linebacker must move in order to tackle the carrier. The slower the ball carrier and the faster the pursuer, the more the defender can move directly at the carrier.

It is of paramount importance that no defenders get behind the ball carrier by penetrating and then have to chase the play.

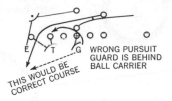

WRONG PURSUIT
GUARD IS BEHIND
BALL CARRIER

THIS WOULD BE CORRECT COURSE

E   T   G

Diagram 8

Instead, the defenders must move on the proper angle of pursuit to get in front of the ball carrier at the earliest possible moment.

HOW TO TACKLE

Having closed on the ball carrier, the defensive player is now ready to make the tackle. As he approaches the area of contact, the defender should bend his knees to assume a balanced base—the hitting position. (See Illustration 2.) His feet should be spread approximately as wide as his shoulders. His eyes must focus on the target, which should be the belt buckle of the ball carrier. (See Illustrations 5

21

and 6.) Most running backs have excellent balance and an uncanny ability to fake with their head, eyes, shoulders, arms and even legs. But it is difficult to fake with the belt buckle. Even O. J. Simpson will be where his belt buckle is. And by concentrating only on the belt buckle, the tackler will avoid being faked.

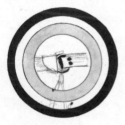

Illus. 5. Tackler's target is the belt buckle.

Illus. 6. Tackler should *not* look at the "whole" ball carrier.

Having assumed the hitting position and keeping his spine straight, his head up and his eyes fixed firmly on the belt buckle, the tackler closes on the ball carrier. At the

Illus. 7A. Tackler ready for contact.

moment of contact, he drives his helmet through the ball as his hands and arms encircle the hips of the ball carrier. By driving the helmet through the ball (held at the runner's

Illus. 7B. Tackler at point of contact.

side), the tackler may knock the ball loose and cause a fumble. The muscles of the tackler's legs, back and arms

Illus. 7C. Tackler lifts ball carrier.

lift the ball carrier off the ground and drive him back so that he cannot fall forward for extra yardage.

The tackler must *never* close his eyes when about to make contact. In the vicinity of the tackler, the ball carrier will be using his most violent evasive moves. If the tackler closes

Illus. 7D. Tackler drives ball carrier back.

his eyes, he is "blind" and hands his adversary a monumental advantage. If he cannot see the ball carrier, the defender has no chance of making a clean tackle.

When the ball carrier is moving at an angle to the outside and it is impossible for the tackler to meet him head on, he should use the side-body tackle. Again, the target remains the belt buckle. At the moment of contact, the tackler again assumes the hitting position. He drives his head and shoulder in front of the ball carrier, grasps him with both arms and then rolls with the ball carrier as he falls forward. If

Illus. 8A. Point of contact for side body tackle.

Illus. 8B. The two illustrations below show tackler rolling with ball carrier.

the tackler's head is not driven across in front of the ball carrier, the carrier's legs, almost certainly stronger than the defender's arms, will enable the carrier to break the tackle and continue downfield. Arm tackling is risky business at best; against the likes of a Larry Csonka or a Larry Brown, it is futile.

Illus. 9A. Tackler using only his arm to try to stop ball carrier.

Illus. 9B. Ball carrier breaks the tackle.

3
Play of the Down (Interior) Linemen

THE PHYSICAL REQUIREMENTS of interior linemen are size, strength and quickness. It is their mission to control the line of scrimmage. They must have sufficient size and strength to be able to defend themselves from the charge of their offensive opponents and not be driven back off the line of scrimmage. *It is one of football's truisms that the team controlling the line of scrimmage wins the game.*

STANCE OF INTERIOR LINEMEN

There are two standard stances for interior linemen, the three-point stance with one hand on the ground and the four-point stance with both hands on the ground. Other than the position of the hands, the stances are identical. (See Illustrations 10 and 11.) To assume a stance, the feet should be spread about the width of the shoulders, the knees bent and the legs coiled. The hips should be

Illus. 10. Three-point defensive stance.

Illus. 11. Four-point defensive stance.

slightly lower than the shoulders and the torso stretched forward, with a reasonable amount of weight on the hand, or hands, on the ground.

Usually the down lineman will crowd the line of scrimmage to get as close to the opponent as the rules allow. However, on occasion, if the defensive man has somewhat slow reflexes, or if he has an assignment to "read" the offense as he charges, he may play back off the line of scrimmage. This gives him a moment to read his key properly before the offensive player can make contact.

In most defensive alignments, the interior linemen are given the responsibility of defeating one opponent and being positive that the opponent does not block them to a particular side. However, while being ready to defeat the primary opponent, the lineman should watch the other two linemen in his immediate area, since any one of the three may attack him. By watching the three men in his area, the lineman gets a fast key to the play being run and is ready to fight the block of the man who is attacking him.

Illus. 12. Defender sees all three men.

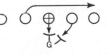

Diagram 9A   Diagram 9B

DEFENDER PROTECTS ONE SIDE

To defeat his opponent and protect his left side, the down lineman charges the opponent with the snap of the ball. He steps with his right foot and drives his right forearm under the chest of the offensive blocker, keeping the blocker's head inside his right upper arm. (See Illustration 13.) He then raises the offensive blocker with his shoulder and forearm, forces him back, frees himself and moves to the ball.

Illus. 13. Defender protects his left side.

To protect to his right, the defender steps with his left foot and hits with his left arm and shoulder.

Some linemen prefer to play with their hands rather than use their forearm as they attack the opponent. For this technique, the foot movement is exactly the same as described above. The heels of the hands drive *under* the shoulders of the offensive player. The hands, arms and back lift the blocker's shoulders and force him back. (See Illustration 14.) This style of charge is difficult for tall men. It also

Illus. 14. Hand shoves defensive charge.

presents the constant danger of the blocker getting under the hands to the body and the legs of the defender. (See Illustration 15.)

Illus. 15. Defender too high. Blocker gets under hands to body.

FIGHT THROUGH PRESSURE

The most important reaction of the defender is to *fight through the pressure of the block*. As he feels which way the offensive man is trying to block him, he must fight that pressure. If he goes *around* the pressure, he will be taking himself out of the play, since he will now be behind the ball.

FIGHT THROUGH
PRESSURE

Diagram 10

NEVER GO AROUND
PRESSURE

Diagram 11

PLAY OF THE NOSE GUARD

The nose guard is a down lineman who plays opposite the offensive center. The basic assignment of the nose guard is to charge and defeat the center, never allowing the center to block him to either side. Some nose guards crowd the ball, which enables them to hit the center as soon as the ball moves. If the nose guard is bigger and stronger than the offensive center, then crowding the line of scrimmage

Illus. 16A. Nose guard crowds the ball.

Illus. 16B. Nose guard back off the line of scrimmage.

is the most effective way to play. However, if the nose guard is not bigger and stronger than the center, he should drop back off the line of scrimmage about 2 feet. This will give him time to read the movements of the guards as he makes his charge against the center. (See Diagrams 9A and B.)

In order to keep the center from blocking him to either side, the nose guard should step with his rear foot, bringing it about parallel with the forward foot as it was in his stance. (See Illustration 17.) He uses the hand lift described above, raising up the center and forcing him back. By having his feet on line and his shoulders parallel to the line of scrimmage, he can successfully fight the pressure of the center's block to the left or the right.

Illus. 17. Nose guard playing the center.

When the down lineman is playing opposite the offensive tight end, his mission is to avoid being blocked in by the end, but, equally important, he must also neutralize the end and keep him on the line of scrimmage. If the end cannot get off the line, he obviously cannot be an effective pass receiver. Also, by controlling and containing the tight end, the defender keeps him from making a double-team block or getting across the line of scrimmage to block a linebacker.

The charge and play of the lineman against a tight end is exactly as described above to defeat a single opponent.

Theoretically, the defense will always have one free man, since only ten offensive players can block when one man has the ball. If a down lineman is able to occupy two offensive players, he will free an additional defensive man. By lining up on the outside shoulder of an opponent or in the gap between two men, the defender can charge either or both of them. And if he can manage to detain both at the line of scrimmage, another defensive man will be freed.

STUNT CHARGES OF INTERIOR LINEMEN

In addition to the basic charge of the down lineman, the defender must know how to execute other defensive charges. If the offensive players are sure that all defensive linemen will simply charge straight ahead, they can block more aggressively and effectively. However, if they are not sure exactly how the defender will move, they must be more cautious in making their charge. By using a variety of charges or "stunts," the defensive man will confuse the blocking assignments of the offense. There are three basic stunt charges: (1) the slant, (2) the loop and (3) the penetrating shoot-the-gap.

Slant charge to the left. The defensive player steps with his right foot, aiming his forearm lift at the far shoulder of the offensive player. The second step with the left foot must get the defender past the head of the blocker. He then parallels

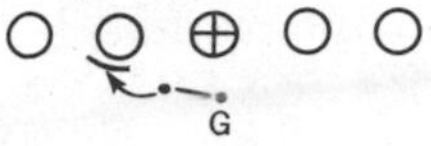

O O ⊕ O O

Diagram 12

his shoulders to the line of scrimmage, finds the ball and
moves to it. The slant charge to the right is made in exactly
the same way, except that the first step is taken with the left
foot.

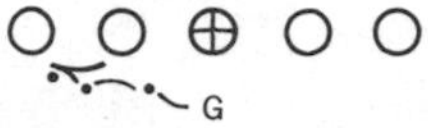

O O ⊕ O O

Diagram 13

Loop charge to the left. The defensive player drops back
off the line of scrimmage about 1½ feet. The purpose of the
charge is to get outside of the offensive player. To loop to the
left, the defender takes a lateral step with his left foot. Without gaining ground forward, he steps beyond his left foot with
his right foot, being certain to get his right arm and shoulder
past the head of the offensive player. He then steps again
with the left foot, parallels his shoulders to the line of
scrimmage, finds the ball and moves to it. The loop charge
to the right is made in exactly the same manner, except that
the first step is taken with the right foot.

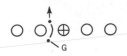

Diagram 14

Shoot-the-gap to the left. When the offensive blockers are
concerned about preventing the slant and loop charges, they
become vulnerable to the quick-penetrating shoot-the-gap
charge. The lineman steps quickly on a 45-degree angle to
the inside, making penetration with his left foot. His left

35

arm and shoulder shield his left hip and leg from the blocker. (See Illustration 18A.) He then steps with his right

Illus. 18A. First step of shoot-the-gap left charge.

Illus. 18B. Second step of shoot-the-gap left charge.

foot to continue to penetrate. By stepping first with the left foot, he will make penetration and be able to place his right foot on the ground to withstand the pressure of the block from his outside. (See Illustration 18B.) Having penetrated, the defensive player finds the ball and moves to it to make the tackle. To shoot the gap to the defender's right, the first step is taken with the right foot.

To summarize: the position taken by down linemen will vary depending on the defensive pattern being used. The linemen will line up on, or slightly off, the line of scrimmage, either head up with an opponent, or shading the outside or inside of an opponent, or in the gap between two offensive linemen. Regardless of the position, or of the charge, the basic fundamentals of each play remain the same. These are:

(1) Take the alignment accurately.
(2) Move with the snap of the ball and execute the basic charge.
(3) Protect the designated area.
(4) Locate the ball.
(5) Pursue the ball on the proper angle.
(6) Make the tackle.

4
Play
of the Defensive Ends

THE PHYSICAL REQUIREMENTS of defensive ends are quickness, speed and body balance. These are the essentials if the defensive end is to avoid being blocked and execute his most important single assignment: that of keeping the ball to his inside on all plays.

STANCE OF DEFENSIVE ENDS

The defensive end uses either a three-point or an erect stance. From the three-point stance (see Illustration 19A),

Illus. 19A. Three-point defensive-end stance.

he is able to make a faster start, since the slight amount of weight on the hand enables him to charge forward more quickly. However, from the erect stance (see Illustration 19B), he gets a better view of the offensive backfield, which enables him to read his key more easily and thereby react more effectively.

Illus. 19B. Erect defensive-end stance.

REACTIONS OF DEFENSIVE ENDS

When the ball moves *toward* the defensive end, he should attack but never allow himself to penetrate *as deep as the ball*. He should try to keep the ball at least 1½ yards deeper in the backfield than his own position. This enables him to meet the blocker and move to the ball regardless of whether the runner moves to his inside or his outside.

Diagram 15

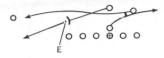

Diagram 16

If the runner moves to the inside, the end should close on him, but always remember that he must maintain outside position as he moves to the ball carrier. If the ball carrier breaks outside of the block, the end, by being closer to the line of scrimmage, can still pursue while remaining outside the ball carrier. His objective should be either to make the tackle or to force the ball carrier out of bounds at the juncture of the line of scrimmage and the sideline. The sideline is the defensive end's ally. By playing as described above, he can force the runner out of bounds at the line of scrimmage whenever the runner breaks outside of the block on the end.

When the ball moves *away* from the defensive end, he must continue across the line of scrimmage until he is as deep as the ball.

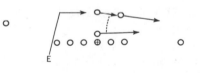

Diagram 17

Having achieved this depth, he should pursue, being certain that he is alert and that his body is under control. By getting this depth, the end will always be able to turn the ball carrier to the inside should a counter play or a delayed reverse develop.

If the end makes the mistake of pursuing too quickly before getting adequate depth, it is possible that a blocker

41

can hit him from the blind side and enable the ball carrier to get to his outside, where there will be no additional defensive support.

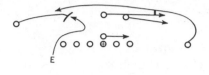

Diagram 18

When the quarterback drops back to pass, the end must rush as quickly as possible. However, he must be certain to maintain outside position on the passer. If he fails, and a blocker hooks him to the inside, the passer can move to the outside to run with the ball. This running threat, exercised so well by quarterbacks like Roger Staubach of Dallas, Bobby Douglas of the Chicago Bears and Greg Landry of the Detroit Lions, breaks down the continuity of the pass defense. Receivers will be open, or the passer will be able to run for considerable yardage. Thus, it is crucial that the defensive end maintain outside position.

STUNT CHARGES OF DEFENSIVE ENDS

In addition to his basic play, the defensive end will be involved in other defensive charges and stunts. On some patterns, he will slash down the line of scrimmage without making any penetration. By doing this, he will unexpectedly force the play at a shallow angle quickly from the outside.

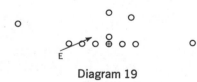

Diagram 19

When he makes this move, his tackle or linebacker will compensate accordingly by looping to the outside and accepting the fundamental responsibilities of the defensive end.

When the defensive quarterback expects the play to be wide to the side of the defensive end, the end's stunt

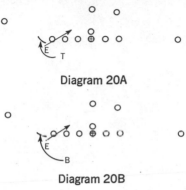

Diagram 20A

Diagram 20B

charge should be to move quickly straight across the line of scrimmage for 5 yards to force the play inside from that point while his teammates pursue from the inside. If the defensive signal-caller has guessed right, in all probability a loss will result.

In long-yardage situations, or when time is running out, the defensive end's charge may be "soft." To execute this, the end takes two short steps back and to the outside as the ball is snapped. He reads the play from this position and pursues accordingly.

To summarize: the assignments of the defensive end on every play are as follows:

(1) Execute the basic charge called.

(2) Always maintain outside position on the ball (unless a stunt charge is called).

(3) Find the ball.

(4) Move on a proper angle of pursuit to the ball.

(5) Make the tackle.

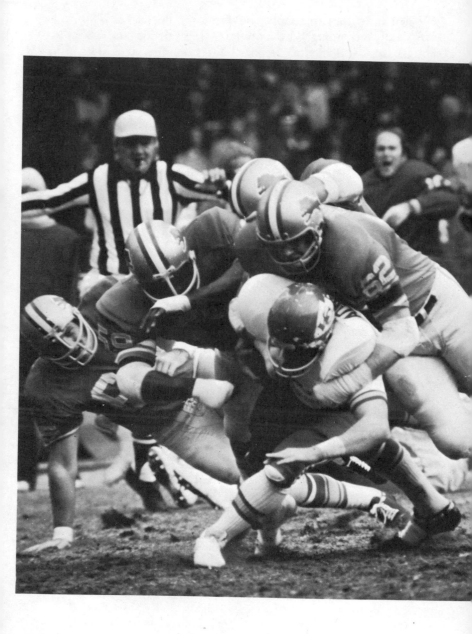

5
Play
of the Linebackers

EVERY DEFENSIVE POSITION is important if the team is to function effectively, but the role of the linebackers is of paramount importance. The linebackers must be strong enough to defeat the blocks of offensive linemen, quick and mobile enough to cover pass receivers and intelligent enough to read their keys quickly and accurately. All in all, it requires splendid all-around athletic ability to play the position effectively. And to see it played by a Dick Butkus of the Chicago Bears today, or by a Joe Schmidt of the Detroit Lions in years past, is to see it played to perfection.

STANCE OF LINEBACKERS

The linebacker's stance should be semierect. (See Illustration 20.) His feet should be spread approximately as wide as his shoulders, with one foot—preferably the outside foot—dropped back slightly. In his stance, the linebacker must

Illus. 20. Stance of defensive linebacker.

have perfect balance so that he can quickly move in any direction.

KEYS OF LINEBACKERS

Usually the linebacker will key on an offensive lineman not covered by one of his own down linemen. The movement of this offensive lineman dictates the reaction of the linebacker. (See Chapter 2, Diagram 5.)

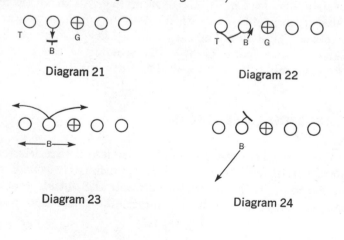

Diagram 21

Diagram 22

Diagram 23

Diagram 24

When the lineman charges at him, the linebacker moves forward to attack using his regular block-protection technique. When the lineman double-teams to either side, the linebacker should move forward quickly to penetrate. He should drive at a point just off the hip of the offensive blocker so that he will not be vulnerable to the trapping lineman moving from that side. When the uncovered lineman pulls to either side, the linebacker moves with him. When the lineman takes a drop step to execute a pass-protection block, the linebacker must drop quickly to his assigned pass-defense zone. While dropping back, he must be alert to the possibility that the pass-protection block is merely a fake to set up the draw play. When this occurs, the linebacker must support quickly against the back who is running with the ball on the draw play.

In each instance, after starting his reaction charge, which is dictated by the movement of the uncovered offensive lineman, the linebacker must find the ball, move to it and make the tackle. When the play is a pass, he covers his zone or the assigned man until the ball is in the air, at which time he again moves quickly to the ball.

STUNT CHARGES OF LINEBACKERS

To confuse the offensive blocking assignments, linebackers must on occasion move as the ball is snapped rather than wait to read their key before charging. The most common stunt charges are in coordination with a defensive lineman or end. If his teammate slants or loops to either side, the linebacker adjusts by moving in the opposite direction to cover the exposed area. (See Diagram 20B.)

If the defensive plan is to have the linebacker penetrate to rush the passer or try to force the play for a loss, he moves opposite to his lineman's charge and penetrates across the line of scrimmage. He then finds the ball and moves to it.

LINEBACKERS' PASS-DEFENSE RESPONSIBILITIES

The linebacker's ability to play effective pass defense is a fundamental ingredient for the success of his team. Generally, he will have two coordinated assignments against pass plays. First, he will always have a designated zone to cover on a pass. (See Diagram 25.) Second, while moving to the zone, he will be responsible for covering a backfield man who may run out to become a receiver.

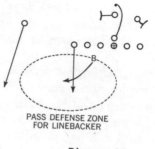

PASS DEFENSE ZONE
FOR LINEBACKER

Diagram 25

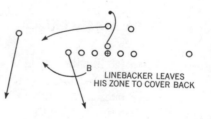

LINEBACKER LEAVES
HIS ZONE TO COVER BACK

Diagram 26

When this happens, the linebacker must leave his zone and cover the back. If his assigned back blocks, he continues to move to his designated pass-defense zone and plays the ball.

It is important that the linebacker get a fast key on pass plays. Most offensive teams will try to disguise their intention to pass, but the uncovered lineman (see Diagram 24) in most instances will quickly indicate to the linebacker whether the play is a pass or a run.

The linebacker should always be conscious of the fact that whenever possible he should delay eligible receivers who start downfield in his area. When the play begins, all of these men are potential blockers, and the rules allow the linebacker to hit them solidly with a block-protection-type blow. If the receiver is moving to the outside, the backer cannot continue to harass him. But if the receiver is moving from the outside in, he remains a blocking threat and the linebacker can, within limits, continue to hit and delay him.

Perhaps the most difficult passes for the defensive team to cover are those that have a receiver crossing the field to the opposite side.

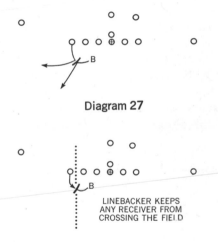

Diagram 27

LINEBACKER KEEPS
ANY RECEIVER FROM
CROSSING THE FIELD

Diagram 28

On plays of this type, the linebacker should imagine that he has the responsibility of creating a wall to prevent any

49

outside receiver from crossing the field to the opposite side.

As soon as they are in position to throw, most passers will look toward the area of the intended receiver. Passers are taught to avoid doing this, but only the highly skilled achieve this discipline in actual game competition. Thus, as the linebacker drops back, he should concentrate on watching the passer (always keeping in mind his responsibility to prevent an eligible receiver from crossing the field).

As the passer starts his throwing motion, the linebacker should immediately break in the direction the ball will be thrown. On drop-back passes, the linebacker should attempt to retreat quickly enough to reach the middle of his zone of protection before the ball is thrown. This spot is approximately 8 to 10 yards back of the line of scrimmage. (See Diagram 25.) If the linebacker does reach his spot of protection prior to the throw of the ball, he should bring his body totally under control and read the passer from a relatively motionless position. By setting up in this manner, he will be able to make a more rapid lateral movement to the side the pass is thrown than is possible if he is dropping back at the time the ball is delivered.

If the linebackers have speed enough to reach their zones and then make the described lateral movement as the ball is thrown, they will establish an effective wall that will require the quarterback to arch the ball over the linebackers in order to hit a receiver who is further than 10 yards

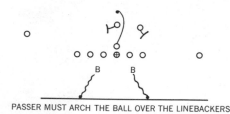

PASSER MUST ARCH THE BALL OVER THE LINEBACKERS

Diagram 29

downfield. When the ball is arched, it takes longer to reach the receivers than when it is "lined." This extra time will give the secondary men the opportunity to move to the ball before it reaches any eligible receiver.

It is of fundamental importance that the linebackers—and all other defensive players—recognize that the rules give both teams an equal right to the ball the moment it is thrown. When the ball leaves the passer's hands, there is no offensive or defensive team, yet many defensive players subconsciously believe that the offense has a prior claim to the ball.

The rules prohibit defensive men from interfering with the receiver's opportunity to catch the ball. They also prohibit the offensive player from interfering with the right of the defensive man to make an interception. If either side is "playing the man," it is guilty of pass interference. (See Illustrations 21 and 22.) If both sides are "playing the ball," they are both within the rules. Thus, when the ball is in the air, the linebackers must go for it with reckless abandon.

Illus. 21. Both men playing the ball legally.

Illus. 22. Player in dark shirt playing Number 11 illegally.

When a pass shows, the linebacker must both play his zone and watch for a delayed receiver coming out of the backfield. (See Diagram 26.) When this situation arises, the linebacker will be playing man-for-man defense. This assignment matches his speed against that of the offensive player, and this once again emphasizes the rigorous physical requirements needed by linebackers. At the business of covering receivers, there are none better than Willie Lanier of the Kansas City Chiefs and Chris Hanburger of the Washington Redskins.

Playing the man-for-man defense is essentially a matter of moving on a proper angle of pursuit. A linebacker must move to the outside rapidly enough to prevent an offensive player from beating him to the outside. If the receiver attempts to break back to the inside, the rules allow the linebacker to maintain his position, and if he is in the right spot, he can legally hit the receiver and prevent him from breaking back to the inside of the field.

52

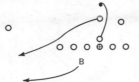

Diagram 30

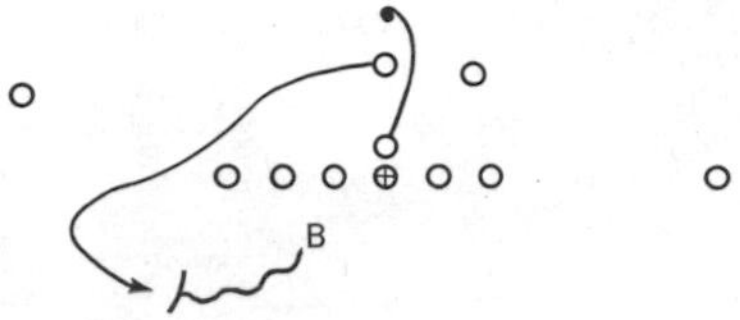

Diagram 31

While moving on the proper angle to cover the potential receiver on the man-for-man assignment, the linebacker should have enough peripheral vision to be aware of the quarterback's movements. He should be especially alert to the moment when the quarterback throws the ball, and as soon as it is in the air, he should release his pursuit of the offensive man and move quickly to the ball.

It is an essential of team defense that all linebackers (and linemen) pursue the ball when it is in the air, regardless of their distance from it. If they stop their pursuit, they become mere spectators. The receiver may catch the ball, avoid the men in his immediate vicinity and break away for a touchdown. If all defensive men are in pursuit, however, someone will usually be able to catch the receiver from behind, since his maneuvering takes time. Thus, defensive pursuit will prevent the touchdown.

6
Play
of the Secondary Men

DEFENSIVE SECONDARY MEN must possess great all-around athletic ability. They must have speed enough to prevent the fastest man on the offensive team from getting behind them on pass plays. They must be tough enough and strong enough to tackle the shiftiest as well as the most powerful running backs. This calls for a rare combination of physical attributes. It calls, at its best, for the likes of a Lem Barney of the Detroit Lions in his prime, or of a Larry Wilson of the Saint Louis Cardinals in his heyday. Or of a Pat Fischer of the Washington Redskins, a Kermit Alexander of the San Francisco 49ers, a Herb Adderly of Green Bay or, if one were to go back a generation, an Emlen Tunnell of the New York Giants.

STANCE OF DEFENSIVE SECONDARY MEN

Regardless of the alignment being played by the secondary, the fundamental techniques for secondary men remain the same. Their stance is similar to that of a linebacker. One foot should be dropped slightly back. The feet should be spread about the width of the shoulders, with the knees bent slightly. The arms hang loosely from the shoulders. (See Illustration 23.) From this stance, the defender will be able to move quickly in any direction.

Illus. 23. Stance of defensive secondary man.

KEYS OF DEFENSIVE SECONDARY MEN

All secondary defenders must think "pass" at the start of each play. They must defend against the possibility of a pass until they are *positive* the play will *not* be a pass. Only two developments after the ball is snapped can give them this certainty:

(1) An offensive lineman (tackle, guard or center) crosses the line of scrimmage and moves downfield.

(2) The ball crosses the line of scrimmage.

When either of these occurs, the secondary men may safely converge on the ball to stop the runner. However, if they gamble that the play is a run and it turns out to be a play-action pass, the receiver may get behind them for an easy touchdown.

In most defensive alignments, the secondary men can look through an uncovered offensive lineman to the ball. By keying on this lineman as the ball is snapped, they get a quick reading as to whether the play will be a pass or a run. This is exactly the same reaction as was described for linebackers in Diagrams 21, 22, 23 and 24.

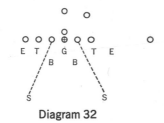

Diagram 32

The paramount mission of the defensive secondary is to prevent the breakaway touchdown. Thus, secondary defenders must coordinate their movements, always keeping the ball in front of and inside of their unit until the tackle is made or the pass broken up.

There are three basic alignments for defensive secondaries: (1) four-deep, (2) three-deep and (3) the "monster" or rover-back pattern. In all three alignments, the basic mission of the unit remains the keeping of the ball inside and in front until the tackle is made.

Secondaries play two types of pass defense: (1) the zone and (2) the man-for-man. In most situations, teams should use the zone pattern since it more effectively prevents breakaway plays.

ZONE PASS DEFENSE

On the zone pattern, all men of the secondary drop back, keeping relative distances between themselves until the ball is thrown. Then they immediately move to the ball. They should read the passer's eyes and try to get the jump on the direction of the pass in exactly the same manner described for linebackers.

If one member of the secondary drops deep while another man fails to drop back, then one deep zone may be left completely open.

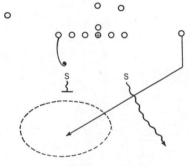

Diagram 33

When playing the zone-type pass defense, the defensive linemen must rush the passer so that he will not have an extraordinarily long time to set up and throw. It is easy to maintain relative position in the secondary for approximately five to six counts after the ball is snapped, but a longer time makes it difficult to hold the pattern and cover the receivers.

MAN-FOR-MAN PASS DEFENSE

When playing the man-for-man pass defense, each eligible receiver is assigned to a particular man in the defensive secondary.

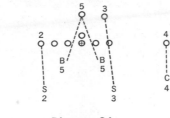

Diagram 34

In the man-for-man defense, a secondary man lines up relatively close to the line of scrimmage. He looks through his receiver to the ball, and when it is snapped he moves with the receiver, keeping him slightly to the inside and 1½ to 2 yards in front of himself. When the ball is thrown, the defender leaves his man and moves to the ball.

Occasionally it is necessary, and tactically sound, for the pass defense to switch secondary men after the ball is snapped. If the tight end breaks on a shallow course to the outside, while the wide receiver breaks on a shallow course to the outside, the coverage is easier if the cornerman and safety "switch" men and cover each other's receiver.

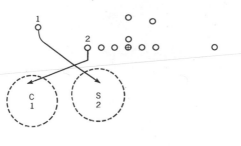

Diagram 35

PLAY OF THE FOUR-DEEP SECONDARY

On the four-deep-zone pass-defense pattern, the entire unit must move together and maintain relative position with each other as they react to the play.

Illus. 24. Four-deep defensive secondary.

(1) When the ball moves to their left, the secondary men rotate in that direction.

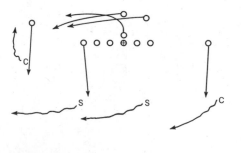

Diagram 36

(2) When the ball moves to their right, they rotate to the right.

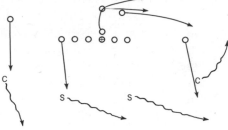

Diagram 37

(3) When the ball moves back, as the passer drops back to get in position to throw, the secondary men also drop back.

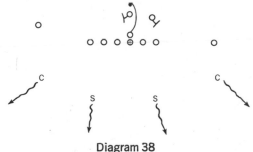

Diagram 38

(4) When the ball moves toward the line of scrimmage, or as on a running play, the secondary men close on it.

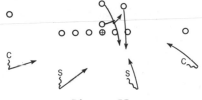

Diagram 39

On all four basic movements, the secondary men must maintain their relative positions with regard to each other as they react to the situation.

PLAY OF THE CORNERMEN
ON THE FOUR-DEEP SECONDARY

When the ball moves to his side, the cornerman reacts as a defensive end would, by coming up quickly to turn the play in. When the ball moves in the opposite direction, the cornerback drops back quickly to become the defensive halfback on his third of the field.

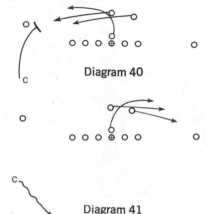

Diagram 40

Diagram 41

When the quarterback drops back to pass, the cornerman should also drop back quickly to cover his assigned pass-defense zone.

One of the great dilemmas for any cornerback is the play which begins as a run to his side but which then sees the quarterback set up quickly to throw a pass. The running fake, which is directed at the cornerback, is the problem. To defend against this type of play, the cornerback should maintain a neutral position until the ball is approximately outside the offensive tackle.

When the ball passes this point to the outside, the cornerman must come up and force the play. If the passer sets up and prepares to throw inside of the imaginary line on Diagram 43, then the cornerback must drop quickly back to cover his assigned outside pass-defense zone.

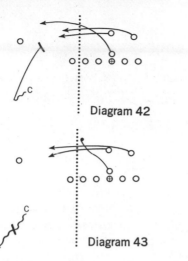

Diagram 42

Diagram 43

The offensive team will present a variety of formations to the cornerman. If the widest receiver is within 8 to 10 yards of the next widest receiver, it is possible for the cornerman to come up on plays in his direction. But if the widest eligible receiver is further to the outside, the cornerman must cover him deep, since the distance is too great for the safetyman to move over quickly enough to cover the receiver who may run a deep outside pattern.

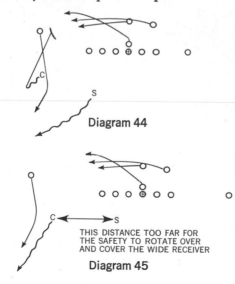

Diagram 44

THIS DISTANCE TOO FAR FOR
THE SAFETY TO ROTATE OVER
AND COVER THE WIDE RECEIVER

Diagram 45

When the widest receiver is out so far that the safetyman cannot possibly get over to cover him, the cornerman's assignment always remains the same: cover the receiver deep.

BUMP-AND-RUN TECHNIQUE

Most receivers run excellent faking patterns, making it difficult for a cornerback to cover them, particularly when the passer can throw especially well. To prevent the receivers from having so much room to maneuver, fake and then make their break into an open area, cornermen occasionally play the "bump-and-run" technique.

To play bump and run, the defender lines up on the inside shoulder of the receiver about 1½ yards from him. (See Illustration 25.) As the ball is snapped, the defender

Illus. 25. Ready to play bump-and-run.

Illus. 26A. The bump.

steps into the receiver, hits him and holds him up. When the receiver gets free, the defender turns and chases him. Obviously, he must possess just as much speed as the receiver if he is to be able to keep him covered as he breaks downfield. The defender watches the receiver as he chases him, and when the receiver looks back to catch the ball, the

Illus. 26B. The run.

Illus. 26C. Playing the ball.

defender also looks back. By concentrating on the man until he looks for the ball, the defender will be able to keep him covered. When the ball is thrown, he will be in the area where it will come down and he will be in position to break up the pass or make the interception.

PLAY OF THE SAFETIES
ON THE FOUR-DEEP SECONDARY

The two inside defenders of a four-deep defense are known as the safetymen. To simplify their assignments, they usually change positions depending on the strength of the offensive formation. Most offensive teams today use one tight end and one split end, who is a wide receiver. The safety who lines up to the side of the tight end is called the "strong" safety, while his colleague who lines up on the side of the split end is called the "free" safety.

The use of the word "free" to describe this man derives from the fact that he has no immediate responsibility for

Diagram 46

Diagram 47

any particular receiver coming deep. He is thus free to roam the secondary and give support where it is most needed.

The two safetymen always react as a team. When the play moves to their side, they move to the outside in that

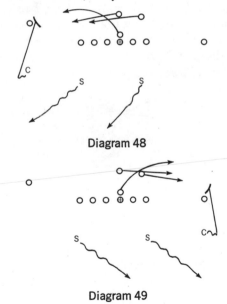

Diagram 48

Diagram 49

direction. As the cornerman comes up, the safety to the side of the play has deep outside responsibility, and the safety-man away from the play has responsibility for covering the deep middle zone.

On drop-back passes, both men move back to cover their assigned zones.

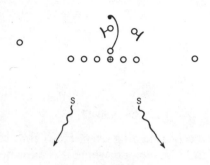

Diagram 50

To change the pace and confuse the offensive blocking, the safetyman may, on a prearranged signal, change assignments with the cornerman. This adjustment is called "inverting." If the play starts to his side, the safetyman comes up immediately to force the play.

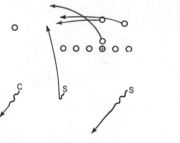

Diagram 51

The cornerman now covers the deep outside, while the safetyman on the side away from the play moves in to cover the deep middle.

68

Both safetymen must recognize the distance the wide receiver is split away from the next widest receiver. When this distance between the receivers is so great that the safetyman cannot get wide enough to cover the wide receiver on a deep outside pattern, the cornerback has the deep outside responsibility. Against such offensive formations, the safetymen will play normally, or invert if the signal has been given to do so, at the snap of the ball.

PLAY OF THE THREE-DEEP
DEFENSIVE SECONDARY

The three-deep secondary is much easier to play since the assignments of the three men involved always remain the same. The two halfbacks must cover the deep outside zones, while the safetyman covers the deep middle.

When the ball moves laterally, the defensive halfback on that side maintains his position 8 to 10 yards deep and

Illus. 27. Three-deep defensive secondary.

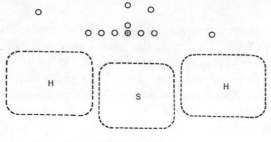

Diagram 52

moves to the outside, playing as though the play will be a pass in his zone, until the ball is thrown or he receives the key that the play is a run instead.

The safetyman gives ground as he moves back with the flow of the play. It is his responsibility to pick up the widest eligible receiver as the halfback maintains the 8- to 10-yard depth. If the receiver is split so wide before the play begins that the safetyman cannot get over to cover him deep, the halfback must take him all the way, exactly as a cornerback does on the four-deep pass defense.

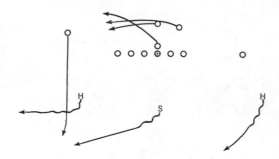

Diagram 53

The halfback away from the flow of the play moves back and slightly to the inside, always being sure that he can cover the widest eligible receiver deep on his side of the field.

On drop-back passes, the three-deep secondary men simply cover their assigned zones of the two outside areas and the deep middle.

PLAY OF THE MONSTER DEFENSIVE SECONDARY

The third pattern of secondary play is the "monster" defense, which is a combination of the three-deep and four-deep patterns. At many colleges employing the rover back, he is given a colorful name. On the Rambling Wreck varsity of Georgia Tech, he is known as the "Wrecker," while the Michigan Wolverines call theirs the "Wolf."

Statistics reveal that the majority of long-gaining offensive plays are directed to the wide side of the field, where there is

Illus. 28. Monster defensive secondary.

more room to operate. The monster defense responds to this by having its extra man play on the wide side of the field on all occasions. (The rare exception to this strategy is when, as a change of pace, the monster may play the narrow side to confuse the offense.)

The monster pattern enables the three-deep defenders to maintain their positions when plays move to the monster's side.

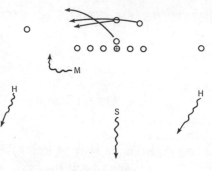

Diagram 54

When the play moves away from the monster man, he moves back to become the defensive middle safety. The safety and halfback to that side react as the safety and cornerman on the four-deep defensive secondary.

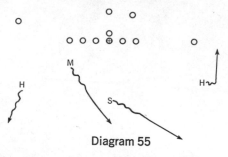

Diagram 55

When the play is a drop-back pass, the monster man can assist in double-covering any dangerous receiver in his area or else relieve the linebacker of the job of covering a backfield man who may come out as a receiver. The flexibility of the monster defense greatly reduces the pressure on the linebackers and secondary, and this is the basic reason why the alignment has been used by so many college teams in recent years.

7
Team
Defensive Alignments

THERE ARE TWO basic types of team defensive alignments: (1) the eight-man front, in which three men play in the secondary, and (2) the seven-man front, with four men playing in the secondary. Each team alignment is composed of down linemen, ends, linebackers and secondary defenders.

BASIC THREE-DEEP DEFENSES

In studying pages 74 and 75, you should note that the only change required to make a 7–1 out of the 5–3 defense is moving up the outside linebackers on the line of scrimmage, where they become down linemen (tackles).

BASIC FOUR-DEEP DEFENSES

In practical terms, a different defensive alignment results by moving a small number of men. (See page 76.) For ex-

Illus. 29. 4–4–3 defensive
alignment.

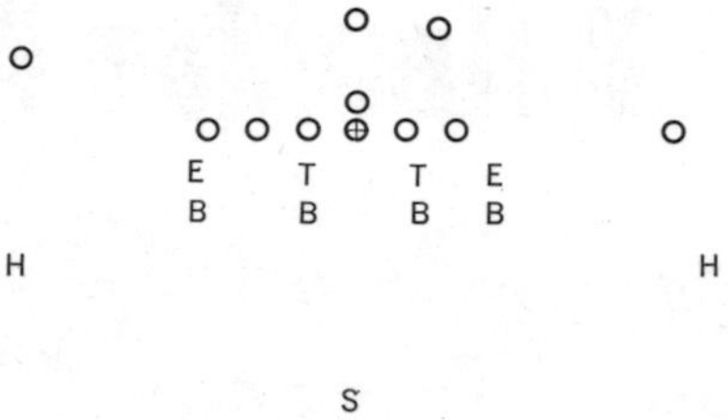

Diagram 56

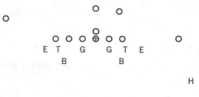

Illus. 30. 6–2–3 defensive
alignment.

Diagram 57

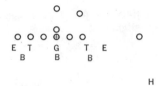

Illus. 31. 5–3–3 defensive
alignment.

Diagram 58

Illus. 32. 7–1–3 defensive
alignment.

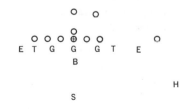

Diagram 59

Illus. 33. 4-3-4 defensive alignment.

```
                    O
                O       O
    O   O   O   O⊕O   O           O
    E   B   T   B T   B   E
    C                           C

        S           S
```

Diagram 60

Illus. 34. 5-2-4 defensive alignment.

```
                O
            O       O
    O   O   O   O   O   O           O
    E   T   B   G   B   T   E
    C                           C

        H                   H
```

Diagram 61

ample, on the 5–2–4, if the nose guard and strong-side down lineman move one man to their right to play opposite the offensive guards, and the linebackers move one man to the opposite side, while the right end drops back to become a linebacker, the 4–3 alignment is created.

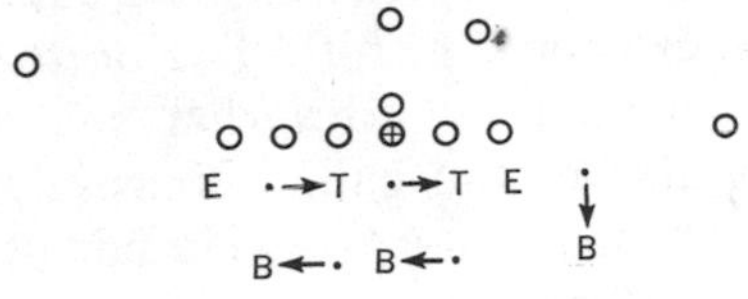

Diagram 62

If the defensive team is in a 4–3 alignment and the down linemen playing on the guards move out over the tackles, the middle linebacker moves up onto the line as a nose guard, and the two outside linebackers move slightly to the inside, then the defense becomes a 5–2.

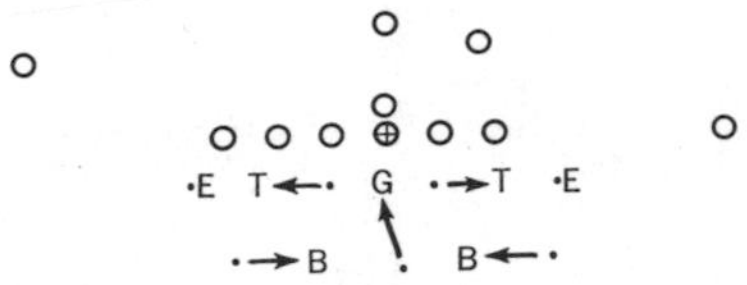

Diagram 63

One of the currently popular defenses in college football, pioneered by the University of Tennessee, is a half 5–2 and half 4–3. The down linemen playing over the tackles on the 5–2 move slightly to the inside and play in the gap between the offensive guard and tackle. The nose guard drops slightly off the line and becomes a linebacker.

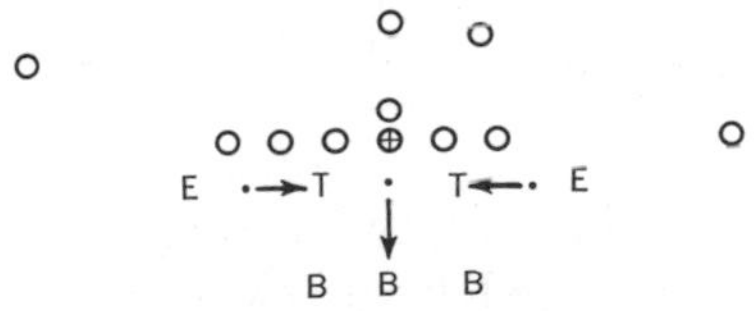

Diagram 64

MONSTER DEFENSES

As was discussed in Chapter 6, the monster defense is actually an overshift, in which the defense commits six men to one side. From the standpoint of the play of the secondary men, it is one-half three-deep and one-half four-deep.

Diagram 65 shows the overshift. The dotted line through the offensive formation indicates that the offense is balanced on either side of the ball. Defensively, the monster man gives his team six men on the wide side of the field with only five to the opposite side.

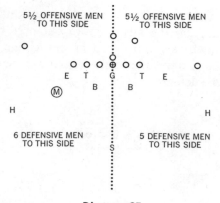

Diagram 65

The monster defense can be used with any variety of alignments by the seven men constituting the linemen and linebackers. It may be a 5–2, 4–3 or any slightly adjusted mixture of the two.

GOAL-LINE DEFENSE

When the offense has the ball within 5 yards of the goal line, the defense is forced to use a goal-line defense. The most commonly used alignment is a 6–5.

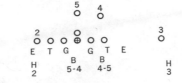

Diagram 66

The six down linemen, ends included, must charge with the snap of the ball, shooting the gap to penetrate as quickly as possible. They must break up the play so that the five linebackers and/or halfbacks can come up fast enough to prevent any gain.

The five secondary men on the goal-line defense usually play man-for-man pass defense as indicated in Diagram 66. If their man comes downfield, they must cover him because of the possibility of a pass. If he blocks, they must come up immediately to support against the run.

The goal line defense is a gamble on the part of the defensive team. The basic rule of the secondary—"keep the ball in front and inside of the unit"—is no longer applicable.

Illus. 35A. Defensive lineman's goal-line defense stance.

Illus. 35B. Goal-line penetrating charge.

Illus. 35C. Lineman shoots gap and gains penetration.

The secondary must therefore take a chance, come up fast and try to prevent the offense from making any yardage, since even a small gain at this spot on the field can be damaging.

PREVENT DEFENSES

When time is running out, either at the half or at the end of the game, and the defensive team is ahead, it is sensible for it to go into a "prevent" defense. It is also a sound strategy on long-yardage situations, regardless of the time remaining.

The purpose of the prevent defense is to ensure that the offense will not be able to break a play for long yardage. There are two standard prevent defenses: the 3–5–3 and the 4–5–2.

Illus. 36A. 3–5–3 prevent defense.

Illus. 36B. 4–5–2 prevent defense.

Most teams using a prevent defense will substitute secondary men for down linemen and linebackers to get maximum speed and mobility. The five linebackers and/or halfbacks on both defenses will play one of two ways: (1) they may play a pure zone, retreating to about 12 to 15 yards behind the line of scrimmage to play the ball, or (2) they may each play man-for-man on the five eligible offensive receivers.

In both defenses, the deep defenders play pure zone while the linemen rush and force the play.

Diagram 67 shows the 3–5–3 alignment with the five linebackers playing pure zone. Diagram 68 shows the 4–5–2 with the five linebackers playing man-for-man.

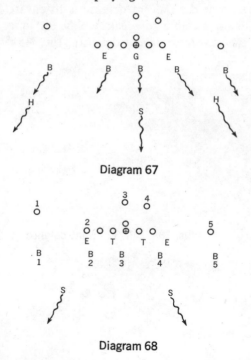

Diagram 67

Diagram 68

8

Defensive Strategy

EFFECTIVE DEFENSIVE FOOTBALL has a direct relationship with the vertical field position of the ball. When the opponents have the ball outside of the defenders' 35-yard line, they have only three downs to make a first down, since they must kick the ball on fourth down or risk surrendering it at that spot.

Diagram 69 shows the three-down and four-down areas of the field from a defensive standpoint. When the offensive team has the ball inside the defenders' 35-yard line, it does not necessarily need to kick on fourth down. Even if the

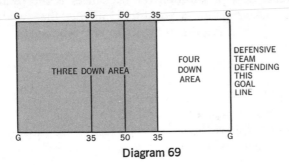

Diagram 69

fourth-down attempt is unsuccessful, it will be surrendering the ball to the opponent deep in his own territory. It will still have field-position advantage. Also, if the offense has an effective field-goal kicker, it may elect to try for the three points on fourth down rather than attempting to make the first down.

IMPORTANCE OF POINT OF EXCHANGE

In planning the tactics and strategy to win a football game, the "point of exchange" is one of the two most important factors in determining the ultimate result. (The other is "time of possession." The team that has possession of the ball the majority of the time usually wins. For example, if our team has the ball for 40 minutes, and the opponents for only 20, our team should win.)

The point of exchange refers to the spot on the field where the offense surrenders the ball to the opponent. The team that has the most favorable field position, cumulatively, on the exchanges will almost always win the game.

For example, if our team gets the ball on the exchange on our own 40, the next time on the opponents' 45, the next time on our 45, and the next time on the opponents' 38, we will be much more likely to win the game than if we get the ball on our own 15-, 22-, 12- or 20-yard lines respectively.

Favorable field position on the exchanges is the result of a strong kicking game, a consistent offense, the avoidance of errors which surrender the ball to the opponents and a solid defense.

The strong kicking game combines the ability to kick the ball out of the end zone on kickoffs, or to kick it high enough and cover so quickly that the opppent is stopped on the return inside of his own 20-to-25-yard line. When forced to punt, it is the ability to make 35 net yards on the play. This requires a punter who can kick well and team speed in covering the kick so no gains can be made on punt returns.

A consistent offense implies the ability to make at least two or three first downs each time a team gains possession of the ball.

The third factor in gaining and maintaining favorable field position is the avoidance of the two major errors of fumbles and pass interceptions. Each time either occurs, the offensive team has surrendered a minimum of the 35 yards it could have made had it punted on the play. The only exception would be a 35- or 40-yard pass interception in which the interceptor is tackled immediately. The net effect here would be the same as if the offense had punted.

Assuming that the ball is in possession of the offensive team in its own territory (the three-down area), the defense has the problem of keeping the offense from averaging 3⅓ yards per play. If the offense makes this much yardage on each of three plays, it will have made a first down. When the ball is in the four-down area of the field, the offense need only average 2½ yards per play.

CREATING OFFENSIVE ERRORS

Assuming sound, consistent execution on the part of the offense, the percentages are in its favor if it avoids errors such as fumbles, interceptions, penalties and assignment mistakes. Most offensive teams can avoid these errors for a limited number of snaps. But the more times it must put the ball in play to score, the greater the odds are that the offense will commit an error. A successful offensive play requires the coordinated execution of eleven men, and this is a difficult feat to achieve for more than six or seven consecutive snaps.

It should be noted here that by far the majority of penalties—some 75 percent—are called against the offensive team. About the only penalties ever called on the defense are roughness, grabbing the face mask, pass interference and an occasional offside. These add up to only one out of four penalties called in an average game; the other three go against the offense.

NECESSITY OF AVOIDING BREAKAWAY PLAYS

The difficulty of the offense in avoiding errors is the prime reason why the point of exchange is so vitally important in the ultimate outcome. If the opponent always gets the ball a long way from the defenders' goal, and if the defenders play soundly by avoiding long gaining plays, the defense will be able to force an error on the part of the offense. This will result in an unfavorable down-and-yardage situation for the offensive team.

It is comparatively easy for the offense to make 3½ yards on any one play. However, if the offense can be forced into a situation where it must make 6 yards or more on a succession of plays to make the first down, the advantage then passes completely to the defense. Thus, a prime objective of the defense must be to create a long-yardage situation. However, there is one prior objective—the avoidance of a breakaway play.

A breakaway play may be defined as one which gains 20 yards or goes all the way for a single-play touchdown. Games of this length can be avoided if the defensive secondary plays correctly and always keeps the ball in front of and inside of its unit. A ball thrown 20 yards or more down the field is in the air long enough for the secondary to get to it and break it up if the members are reading their pass keys properly.

Breakaway plays result from errors by the secondary. If this unit executes its basic objective and gets reasonable support from the linemen and linebackers, no breakaway plays can be made.

HOW TO CREATE A LONG-YARDAGE SITUATION

With the secondary playing errorlessly, it now becomes the mission of the linemen and linebackers to create a long-yardage situation. Such a situation is defined as one requiring the offense to average 6 yards on a successive series of plays to make a first down. Long-yardage situations are created by:

(1) A penalty against the offensive team.

(2) An offensive ball-handling error resulting in a loss on the play.

(3) An offensive assignment error enabling the defensive player to make the tackle behind the line of scrimmage for a loss.

(4) A well-executed defensive maneuver by the linemen and linebackers resulting in a loss of yardage on the play.

It may appear to be negative thinking to assume that the opponent will be penalized so that the defensive team is presented with a long-yardage situation. But it remains a fact that the vast majority of offensive teams will incur a penalty if they are required to put the ball in play fifteen or twenty consecutive times. Some offensive player will hold, jump offside, clip, etc. Thus, a defensive team that plays sound field-position football by always making the point of exchange deep in the opponent's territory can, except against a truly excellent opponent, expect to get a long-yardage situation as a result of a penalty if the team combines perfect defense against breakaway plays with excellent field position at the point of exchange.

The same thing is true of backfield ball-handling errors. While offensive teams are expected to handle the ball flawlessly, the fact remains that if they are required to put the ball in play a number of times in succession, sooner or later someone will mishandle it. And even though the offense may recover its fumble, yardage will be lost on the play and a long-yardage situation will be created.

All offensive linemen have blocking rules which, if properly followed, will have each man taking out an assigned defender. Again, while mistakes should not occur, the defense can sooner or later expect to force an offensive error if it plays intelligently and varies its alignments. Then the defenders will (1) move in, (2) throw the ball carrier for a loss and (3) once again create their coveted long-yardage situation.

TEAM DEFENSIVE STUNTS

The preceding three means of creating a long-yardage situation require the cooperation of the offensive team. Excellent opponents—and there are very few of these in actual competition—will not make these self-defeating errors. Against such good teams, it will be necessary for the defense to employ a stunt that will enable it to penetrate behind the line of scrimmage and throw the ball carrier for a loss. Such stunts are relatively simple to execute and are a combination of a slant or loop charge by a lineman or end and a "read-key" by the linebacker. (See Diagram 20B.)

There are almost unlimited numbers of ways these combinations of line charges and keying by linebackers put pressure on the offense.

Diagram 70A shows the linemen slanting to their right. The left end must step with his right foot and hold up the offensive tight end so that he cannot block on a linebacker. If the ball moves to the right, as diagramed, the right-side linebacker will shoot the gap between the guard and the tackle. Four men are now penetrating if the play goes this way, and a loss is almost sure to result. The left-side linebacker, by reading his key (the side to which the ball is going), simply moves to his right and plays as a regular linebacker.

If the play goes away from the slanting linemen, the defense is still sound, as is shown in Diagram 70B. The linemen are slanting to the right, but the play goes to

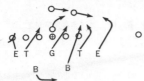

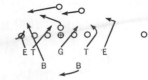

Diagram 70A

Diagram 70B

their left. This changes the key of the linebackers. When the ball moves to the left, the left-side linebacker shoots the gap just outside the offensive tackle. This charge, coupled with the slant of the lineman on the tackle, has two men penetrating on this side. The right linebacker, also by reading the key (the side to which the ball goes), moves to his left to support normally.

Diagram 71A has the linemen slanting to the *left*, the ball moving to the left and the linebackers using the same keys described above. The left linebacker shoots the gap between the guard and tackle, giving four-man penetration on that side. The right linebacker reacts normally, moving to his left. Diagram 71B has the linemen slanting to the left and the ball moving to the right. By shooting the gap outside the offensive tackle, the right linebacker may get through. The left linebacker supports normally.

Diagram 71A

Diagram 71B

By using defensive stunts of this kind, particularly when a running play is expected, it is possible to break into the backfield and stop the ball carrier for a loss. Such maneuvers weaken the pass defense, but the unexpected rush of the linebackers may enable a defensive player to get to the passer before he can throw and thus again create the long-yardage situation.

VARYING DEFENSIVE PLAYS FOR DIFFERENT DOWN-AND-DISTANCE SITUATIONS

On every play, all defensive men must be conscious of the "down-and-distance" situation. This means that they must be aware of the yardage needed by the offensive team to make a first down and thereby retain possession of the ball.

Once a long-yardage situation has been achieved, the objectives of the defense change. When a second-down-and-15-yards-to-gain situation has been created, the defense can allow the offense to make 7 yards on the next two plays (if it is in the three-down area of the field) and still force it to surrender the ball.

In such situations, the defense should not attempt to *force* the play with so much vigor that it loses the swarming effect of every man being part of the pursuit pattern. The defensive players should all think: "We can let them make 5 or 6 yards on this play and still be in control of the situation." This mental adjustment will make it extremely difficult for the offense to make the first down.

There is a difference of opinion among coaches about how to handle short-yardage situations in the three-down area of the field. Some believe it best to go into a goal-line defense in an attempt to stop the opponents for no gain. Others fear that this commitment results in too great a risk and that a breakaway play may result from the overcommitment.

Assuming relatively equal personnel offensively and defensively, percentages dictate that the defensive team should not overcommit on short-yardage situations in the three-down area of the field. Teams that prevent their opponents from making more than 15 yards on any one play during a game are rarely defeated. By combining the sound defensive plan outlined above, waiting for an offensive error and limiting the offense to relatively short gains, the percentages will favor the defensive team that does not overcommit on a short-yardage situation. If the offense does make the first down, it is still in the three-down area of the field and the defense can still hope to force an error.

9

Coordinated Defensive Plan

ALL FOOTBALL FOLLOWERS recognize that the offensive team has a variety of plays from each of its formations. An offensive team must be able to run inside or outside, pass effectively and employ deception and misdirection maneuvers.

To play sound defensive football, the defensive team must also have a coordinated plan. From any alignment, it must have plays that will stop the offense cold if the defensive quarterback has guessed the point of attack. The game is a continual matching of strategy and tactics between the offensive and defensive signal callers.

Diagram 72 shows the 5–2–4 defense being played nor-

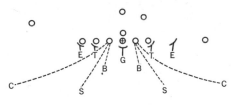

Diagram 72

mally with all men executing their basic assignments and reading their keys.

Diagram 73 shows the ends and tackles shooting to the inside as the linebackers react normally. This maneuver should stop all inside plays for no gain or a loss.

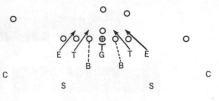

Diagram 73

Diagram 74A shows the linemen slanting to the right and the linebackers keying normally. This maneuver should stop any play moving to the right for a loss. Diagram 74B shows the linemen slanting to the left and the linebackers keying normally. If the play goes to the left, it should be stopped, or thrown for a loss.

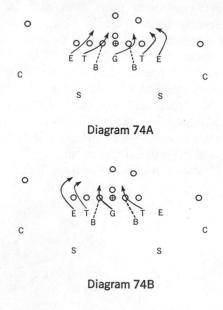

Diagram 74A

Diagram 74B

If a pass is expected, by executing the defensive play in Diagram 75, all receivers will be covered effectively and a pass should be impossible to complete.

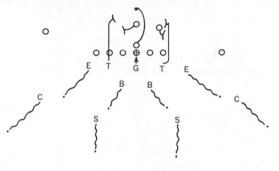

Diagram 75

If a pass is anticipated and the defensive quarterback believes that a strong rush, or "blitz," should be employed to hurry the passer, the maneuver outlined in Diagram 76 should enable one of the linebackers or linemen to get to the passer.

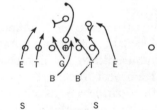

Diagram 76

CHANGING THE DEFENSIVE ALIGNMENT

Even though the defensive plays described above put pressure on the offensive team, a well-organized offense will be able to do an effective job of picking up the stunts. To add further confusion for the offensive blockers, the defense should continually alter its alignment. This will require the offensive linemen constantly to readjust their blocking assignments and increase the possibility of mistakes.

From the 5–2 front, the nose guard and the right down lineman can move half a man to their left, lining up in the gaps. The linebackers play directly behind them. From this alignment, the down linemen can charge back to their original positions, shoot the gap in front of them or charge

Diagram 77

to their right while the linebackers step left as they read their regular key. This adjustment does not require any time-consuming coaching or special preparation by the defensive team. This so-called "stack" alignment puts great pressure on the offensive linemen by confusing their blocking assignments.

Offensive teams that take an inordinate amount of time to call the snap signal after setting up at the line of scrimmage may be vulnerable to a quick change of position by the defensive team just before the snap. Most offensive teams instruct the quarterback to look over the defense and occasionally call a new play—the so-called "audible"—at the line of scrimmage if he thinks that the defense might have successfully anticipated his original play. If the defense continues to jump about at this time, it will further confuse both the quarterback and the offensive linemen, who will be forced to readjust their blocking assignments.

94

10
Summary

AS NOTED at the beginning of this book, effective defensive team play is the key to victory. A team must stop the opponent and gain possession of the ball before it can use its own offense.

Since the offense possesses the initiative, knowing the formation it will use, the play it will run and the moment the ball will be snapped, the defense is at a disadvantage when the play begins. It takes great athletic ability to offset these advantages of the offense.

Since, as stated earlier, most of the publicity and glamour surrounding a football team is focused on the offensive players, particularly the backs and pass receivers, the coach's use of his most talented athletes on defense can create a morale problem.

In its pure sense, the ego of the players dictates that talented backs and receivers would prefer to play offense, where they will get maximum publicity. Talented linemen may prefer to play defense, since they usually will gain more notice from making a tackle than for making an effective block.

To offset these obvious areas of self-interest, it is absolutely necessary that the coach be able to convince his players that they must all use their best talents to further the success of the team.

An outstanding example of this is the case of Allen Lowery of the University of Texas. In 1970 and 1971, he was a starting defensive halfback on the great Longhorn teams that won the Southwest Conference Championship. Few football fans—even the most avid Texas followers—gave Lowery adequate credit for his contribution to the success of the team.

In 1972, Lowery was shifted to quarterback, where he immediately became an outstanding player in the most publicized offensive position. He guided the Longhorns to the Southwest Conference Championship and a victory over Alabama in the Cotton Bowl game. These exploits made his name a household word, not only in Texas, but also in the homes of football fans throughout the nation.

Any football team that is to have consistent success must begin by playing effective defense. The coach must be able to convince all members of the team of the necessity of having the most highly skilled athletes play defense, where their play will gain ball possession for the team. Unless skilled athletes like Lowery are willing to forget personal ambition and play defense, it is impossible for a team to play to its full potential. Effective defense is the only sure road to victory.